MW01275019

// beautifully broken

a rhythmic inner monologue

// beautifully broken

a rhythmic inner monologue

gabrielle lussier

beautifully broken:
a rythmic inner monologue
copyright © 2019 by Gabrielle Lussier

All rights reserved.
This book or any portion thereof may not be reproduced or used in any manner
whatsoever without the express written permission of the publisher or author.
However, you are encouraged to take photos, and post them to social media.
Be sure to tag the author in all such posts, @gbrielle.olivia

Independently published
through Amazon's Kindle Direct Publishing

First Printing, 2019

ISBN 978-1-0901-6332-5

Cover art by Gabrielle Lussier
Interior text design by Gabrielle Lussier

Does anyone ever read this?
If you read this far I just want you to know that
you're amazing and my favourite person ever.

www.gabriellelussier.com
Contact Gabrielle at hello@gabriellelussier.com

//

for anyone who has ever been lost,
I wrote this for you—
but I also wrote this for me.

v

table of contents

// 144

hi, my name is gabrielle and I've fallen in love with the constellations of the night sky because they're the only things I know will never leave me. my hobbies include eating tomato soup, walking barefoot through the grass, falling asleep on the couch, letting my dog lick my face, and writing poetry— but I would never call myself a poet. I also forget to eat dinner, cry myself to sleep more times than I like to admit, and read two thirds of books because I lose hope that the ending is as good as the beginning. I'm too timid, too cautious, my soul has callouses from rejection but they're not yet rough enough to protect. I deal with depression, and I'm still learning how to let sadness be a part of me without consuming my identity completely. there are 57 pairs of shoes in my closet but I never feel comfortable standing on my own two feet. hearing my voice out loud sounds like a stranger whispering my secrets to a room of crowded people. one day I'll stand with my shoulders straight, and share these words with someone else, but my story hasn't started yet.

//

the dark.

// 65

it's 12:39 AM
and I'm crying over somebody
who never loved me
and never planned to.
but truthfully
when I look deep down
I'm crying because of the fear I hold
deep in my soul
about never being wanted
of being unlovable
that this broken brain
is too full of sorrow
to be considered beautiful.

// 173

I can tell it's a low day
when even the most inconsequential things annoy me
like when my thighs stick to the leather of the car seat
or when the brakes are too touchy
or when the light turns red
or when i can't bear the thought of dying
or when dying seems like an option
don't get me wrong I'm not suicidal
but sometimes I wonder what it would be like to disap-
pear for a while
call me sleeping beauty
don't wake me up with a kiss
wake we up with a new brain
this one's broken
did I mention I like to complain
these poems could go on forever notice how my
writing's getting messier

I'm an explosion of unfinished thoughts

have you ever felt like you're on borrowed time
like your mind and body don't want to align
my knees are jittery but my thoughts are calm
or my legs need rest but
my head just won't stop spinning
are your thoughts too loud?
mine need to learn to use their inside voices
it's hard to make anything out amidst all this shouting

I cried in my car this morning.

// 172

once a month I have to visit the pharmacy
where white coats
prescribe me happiness in a bottle
and before that
every two weeks
I had to see a doctor with round glasses
listen to me explain
the darkness in my head
and he would scribble a new antidote
for me to try
now i'm on antipsychotics
instead of antidepressants
and somehow
I feel even more broken
even though this is the first part of being
sewn back to together
sometimes I feel sorry for myself
that my body isn't able to manufacture
something other bodies–other factories
make for free
so easily
I have to import mine
and it comes with duties
taxes and tarifs
in the form of nausea,
hair loss, weight gain and
dizziness
talk to your doctor to see if bipolar disorder
is right for you
every night i get a chalky pill

stuck in the back of my mouth
feels like i've managed to swallow a toad
ever feel like you've got a frog in your throat?
cat got your tongue?
I should probably hold mine
first dates don't go so well when you use the words
'cyclical mood disorder'
when they ask you to describe yourself in three words
but I've kept this darkness inside of me
for so long
letting it out feels like popping the cork
off an expensive champagne bottle–so satisfying
and who said I can't celebrate every part of my identity
because honestly
sometimes I'm scared
that when I'm medicated
I'll lose all creativity
because on the low days
words flow freely
making art is easy
tears paint the most beautiful pictures
who decided poetry has to be angry?
on one hand
I'm joyful that my mood is stabilizing
but on the other
I mourn the loss of inspiration
because even though I deal with depression
I'm still learning how to let sadness be a part of me
without consuming my identity completely

I guess i need to find new things to write about.

// 157

and then she realized
that the numbness
is almost as bad
as the pain.

// 131

now I'm sitting on the couch in my work shirt
and I can't go to work
but I really want to go to work
because lately I feel like I only
ever let people down and most of all me.
because have you ever slept the day away
because your head is fuzzy
like the radio is just off of the channel
you want to listen to
so you kind of hear your favourite song but you
know how much better it really sounds,
that's the way my life is lately
I can tell something's
just not quite right
and that something is me.
now my dog is whining
and he needs to go outside
but that means washing the tear stains off
of my work shirt
which reminds me that I should
probably call in sick
because no one is going
to buy a computer from the sobbing girl
in the corner
I wish I was invisible
yet I wish
I was invincible
but I also wish someone would
ask me what was wrong
but then I'd have to
practice my answer because I don't even know
I can't tie my story into a neat little bow

I'm messy overflowing
coloured outside the lines
slanted handwriting
dirty laundry on the floor
my dog is still whining.
I'm still wearing my work shirt.
I'm still glued to the couch like my legs
are made of cement all I want to do is sleep
but I feel guilty
for not being able to do things
that normal people find so easy like
getting up off the couch
to call in sick to work
but then I'd probably have to make up
a story like I have a headache or homework
because normal people
don't start crying for no reason
and normal people don't have to
sleep all day
and normal people don't feel awful
over the fact that they had to call in sick
and normal people don't wonder
if their managers are suspicious
and normal people colour inside the lines.
I hate normal people.
my dog knows something is wrong
and he's starting to lick the tears off of my cheek
as if to say
stop feeling sorry for yourself
now let's get some fresh air
the dog is me I'm talking
to myself again.
I should probably take off my work shirt.

// 159

sometimes I reread
old poems
and I'm surprised
to find sorrow
behind cobwebs
in corners I didn't know
existed.

// 193

they say diamonds
are made under pressure
mined from the earth's crust
but you know what else
is made from pressure?
dust.

// 40

thoughts, head
tangly mess
lights off
clothes, undress
window open
street sounds
light, sneaks in
night surrounds
sleep, remote
your name, can't grasp
personality, snake
poison, antidote
gasp

// 194

mom asks me
when are you going to write about hope?
well,
I slept until 4 pm today
getting up was too much effort
yesterday I pierced my own ear
twice.
to see if pain was still a long lost friend
he was.

I get tattoos
to remind myself
that this body is mine
so I can't mistake it for someone else

every so often I don't recognize
my eyes in the mirror.
you know that feeling of listening
to yourself on tape?

I don't recognize her voice.

pounding temples makes hearing
my tangled thoughts impossible.
good thing I can read my own lips.

hope?

I'm sure she's off somewhere, hiding.
don't get me wrong.
I've never stopped looking for her.
but I get scared when instead of dust bunnies
l find monsters under the bed.
sometimes you get tired of looking.
hope for me is normalcy
hope is this dream of not needing pills
hope is wishing I was born a different person
maybe hope is inside of me?
right now hope feels like a
lofty sky high atmosphere thousands
of light years away
she's out of my grasp.
my family offers to send out a search party.
looking for the girl they knew decades ago.

maybe I need to lower my expectations.

// 105

she wants more flesh
on her bones while I wish
my butcher had trimmed
the fat,

I am no lean cut of meat.

// 117

it's really hard
being upset
when you don't know
why you're upset
how do you stop crying
when you don't know why
the tears are falling
in the first place.

// 51

I know I'm good enough
but why do you make me
feel like I'm not
good enough for you.
I know I should be happy
but why aren't I smiling
unless we're talking
with each other
why do I only
laugh at your jokes
when mine are much
funnier.

good enough for you

I know I should be happy
but why aren't I smiling

// 70

I feel anchors on my lips
pulling down the corners of my mouth
no one will be able to
catch a smile today.

go on.
cast the net.
my laugh is an
endangered species.

// 54

how is it possible
that I can be so lonely
in a city of just under a million
surrounded by people
just as lonely
as I am.

// 133

today I wondered
what my reflection would be
if I looked into a pool
of tears I've cried
how many of them
were over spilled milk.
I guess if they hadn't been shed
I wouldn't have these
wrinkles in my hands,
the same determination
in my eyes,
the vivid dreams
in my head.

// 109

sometimes,
at night,
I forget what my
voice sounds like.

// 98

why is it so much easier
to talk about the rain clouds
than the sunshine
remember the hurricane
and not the gentle breeze
why do I remember the tidal waves
like they happened yesterday
but recall the quiet creek
as a remnant of a dream.

// 198

you don't have
a monopoly on pain
just because your
stitches run deeper
doesn't mean I'm not
allowed to complain
if that were true
you wouldn't be able
to smile on account
of my laugh being louder.

// 147

if you're used to equating
happiness with
temporary
what do you do when the smiles
don't go away
when the laughter is
here to stay?
but you're terrified
to admit it
because this is the most normal
you've felt in what feels
like a millenia
when you're not used
to being awake
in the daytime
when you're not used to
finding clarity
when you need it
when you're not used to
this thing called focus
when the tears aren't daily
or always
or frequent
instead they're seldom
sometimes
distant.
and let me tell you
happy tears feel
so much better
than the sad ones.

// 126

sometimes I wonder
what it's like
to feel normal
every day
because these
less-than-normal days
are really starting to
bring me down
but then I remember
that if everyday were normal
I probably would write less
and be a little different
than the person I am today
and that makes me sad
so for now I'll deal
with the depressed
and the lonely
and the darkness
because when the sun
finally rises
the light seems to shine
a whole lot brighter.

// 155

sometimes I wonder
why I didn't realize
something was so wrong
I guess when you're
stuck in a tidal wave
you don't know how
fast you're going
until you go
crashing into shore.
when you're in the middle
of a tornado
everything seems calm
until you stop spinning
long enough to see the wreckage.
I was the wreckage.
I was a tornado of tidal waves
one disaster just isn't
enough destruction
tongue of sharpened shells
shoulders weighed down by heavy sand
hair made of tunnel clouds
mirrors broke out of fear
when they saw me
7 years of bad luck
on top of being ugly
mood swings as high and low

as the changing tide
meltdowns a tsunami
of tears
no wonder I didn't
feel close to my friends
I had washed them all away.
thank goodness they never stopped swimming.
lately I've been finding life jackets
in the smiles of strangers
and sometimes your voice
drowns out the whistling of the wind.
if I stand still long enough
sunlight starts to break through
the storm clouds
but I'm too cynical to ever look for a rainbow.
I'm still not convinced my story has a happy ending.
I'm too scared I'll jinx it.

// 101

when the pain is constant
its absence feels like pleasure.
I'm waiting for the pause.

// 114

someone with a broken leg
says they're in pain,
no one questions it.
but as soon as I say
I'm having a bad night
something must
be to blame.
I'm tired of having
to make up reasons
as to why
I'm sad.

// 154

and the sad thing is,
tears feel like a long lost friend.

// 149

you walk around
like you own the word
'depressed'
as though it's no more
than a synonym for sadness
I don't own a thesaurus
because "depressed,"
well,
somedays it owns me
because I'm bound with shackles
to my
prescription bottles
and bed sheets
invisible handcuffs
and emptiness
tie me down
you don't know depressed
like I do.

// 161

how does this shirt look
I ask
sister says
it doesn't show off your waist
as if being skinny
is the only thing worth
being good at
how do these pants look
I ask
mother says
your legs look like sausages
I feel my legs burn
like they were tossed in
a deep fryer
I'll never forgot how much
the hot oil words stung.
dad, I got a tattoo
apparently that's
the Worst thing a daughter could do.
I'll never forget that look
of disappointment.
my mom's so happy I'm
trying to lose weight.
because looking good in the pictures
is more important than
the way your body feels
in the moment.
fitting into that dress
is worth kilograms of self esteem
but not too much
you don't want it to
start weighing yourself down.

// 99

some days,
words aren't enough.

// 41

voice bitter
lemon and acid
mixed to put holes
through my
notion of who
we were
together
but no longer two
one and one
I gather
we're separate
from now on.

// 93

how many prescription drugs
will it take for me to feel well again
how many doctors appointments
psychiatric evaluations
specialist's offices
until someone's able to
fix this broken brain.

// 85

filled to the brim
I contain my emotions
don't feel them
until they overflow

in the shape of
tears

running

down

my

cheeks.

// **32**

some days I wake
and it feels like
he's gone
but in reality
he's just on vacation
lulling me into this
false sense of security
and just when I forget
what sadness feels like
he's back
and this time
he's brought friends.

// 46

alarms silent
curtains closed
makeup on
still dressed in the clothes
from the previous day
lying awake
on top of the covers
most of the time
the smallest endeavours
take the most effort
when your head
is a black cloud
and your chest
concave
un-proud.

// 141

I've kept it in
for exactly
nine days
but tonight
I finally
let myself
cry
over you.

// 156

tonight I'm going to whisper
my fears into my hot chocolate
while falling asleep on the couch
wishing I was anywhere
but here.

// **84**

my eyes are
leaking tonight.

// 79

my depression manifests
in unanswered texts
month old laundry
dirty dishes
nervous ticks
sleepless nights
sleepy days
eyes drifting
voice wandering
ears ringing
saying one thing
but meaning another
tears escaping when
I'm trying to hold them
prisoner.
hopelessness
masking insecurities
with new jeans
and loose clothes
foundation to
cover blemishes
baseball cap
to cover greasy hair
there are signs
but you have
to be willing to
read the map.

//160

I walked to a coffee-shop
because I felt like crying
it's funny how
strangers keep the
tears at bay
here's a tip:
grow bangs so that
people have to look harder
to see your eyes.

// 78

laying in the blackness
waiting for the cough syrup.

// 31

silence suffocating
quiet comforting
solitude stifling
friends misunderstanding
noise aggravating
clock ticking
time slowing
day passing
sleep encompassing
tears trickling
pillow muffling
voice silencing.

// 107

my poetry always
sounds better at night
something about
the way words
sound in the dark
maybe it's because
I'm delirious from
lack of sleep
or maybe it's because
the sunlight brings out
the worst of
my insecurities.

// 102

even when she smiles
there's a twinge of sadness
hidden in the apples
of her cheeks,
bittersweet.

// 130

every task
seems insurmountable lately
getting out from under these covers
is climbing everest
putting on jeans is
slipping down an icy face
walking out the door is
too much work my rope keeps fraying
here I am
down at the bottom again,

I'm staying.

// 119

today,
I need an extra
amount of
kindness.

// 115

tear stained pillow
I cried myself to sleep again
this routine is becoming
all too familiar.

// 77

why is it that
when I need sleep the most
he's unreachable
untouchable
a current of air I just can't grasp
brushing my cheek, teasing
before flitting out my bedroom door
vacating the building
now I'm alone in my bed
eyes open wide awake
my soul heavy ready for sleep
but he doesn't come back
I can hear him outside my window
he's rustling through trees
whipping around corners
and he'll come to me when I
least expect it
so for now all I can do
is wait.

// 87

over the years,
I've learned
how to hide the tears.
running water,
sound of dirty dishes
turn the fan on high,
loud whirring
pretend to yawn,
explain away the redness
look away, pretend to see
something in the distance
dim the lights,
shadows hide the sadness.

// 47

when I am sad I turn off the lights
because that's what I'm supposed to do.
darkness feeds on the sadness
or is it the other way around.
why do I feel like my head has to lay on a pillow
before I'm allowed to cry
allowed to feel.
because this darkness is inside of me
but I never get to let it out
because no one knows it's there
so I guess that's why the night sky is my friend
the moon is my companion who I tell
all of my worries to
she listens patiently but never offers me advice
because that's not why she's there
she's there to give off just enough light
to remind me that there exists a place
much different than my bedroom
much different than the space I inhabit
where I have to squint to see my hand in front of me
maybe that's why I like it so much
my body flows seamlessly into the dark corners
under the covers
moving freely without being seen
my outsides
finally match
my insides.

...way around...

...feel like my...

...I'm allowed...cry...

...allowed to f...

...because...his da...inside of...

...but I nev...ge...at...

...because no one...ther...

...I g...es...that...ght s...is...

...hea...it is...who I te...

...he...never offers...

...b...she's there...

...enough ligh...

...exists a p...

...my bedr...

...t than the s...

...squint...

// 175

I could hear the distance
in their voices.

// 199

darkness has
found a home in me.
no wonder I've always
been a night owl.

// 177

I was all of sadness
mostly lonely
frequently empty
sometimes anxious
never myself.
now I've left those emotions behind me
swept under the rug
they're still there,
peering from the doorway

but they don't recognize me
anymore.

// **118**

how often are
these words
disguised
cries
for help.

// 24

my head is a black cloud
messy scribbles
a host of anticipation
tense with apprehension
the slightest event
can become a trigger
you not answering
makes me question my
self worth
why am I not good enough
a negative interaction
becomes my fault
what could I have done
to prevent it
a simple comment
twists until it has morphed
into an ugly
nasty
insult.

// 203

I'm sinking
to the bottom
I'm a nervous wreck
can't hold my breath
this long
never learned to
deep sea dive
maybe someone will
find this treasure chest
of mine.

// 204

can you even hear me?

//

the light.

// 197

this year
I've said goodbye.
I've sighed.
because of sadness. exasperation.
over little things. out of frustration.
but just as all good things
must come to an end,
so do bad things.
and looking ahead
I see more joy tha I've ever seen before.
I see hellos—I see smiles
I see a face I haven't seen for a while
mainly my own—looking happy.
so here's to a new year with fewer tears
and more laughter.
to overcoming fears
to seeing beyond the horizon.
because I've been through hell and back
but I've learned that I always
cross the finish line more or less intact.

// 81

I can't remember
the last time
my mind
was so clear.

I am a moonlit whirlpool
crystal daggers
blindingly beautiful
and oh so dangerous.

// 166

is it just me
or do some days
colours seem brighter.

// 76

whoever said
'beauty is in the eye
of the beholder'
didn't have the
same insecurities I do
it's not up to you
to decide my worth
it should read
'beauty is in the eye
of the owner'
because I'm always
going to choose
self love over
your cold shoulder.

// 188

when you finish a book
and stare at that last letter
hoping there's another chapter,
but then you realize
that when it's closed
you can feel the weight of the pages
between your palms
see the space it takes up
on your bookshelf.

just look at what
you've accomplished.

sunlight flies in
glass unstoppable
blinds crackable

———————————
———————————
———————————

bed comfort
than the promise
of fresh starts.

// 18

sunlight flies in
glass unstoppable
blinds crackable
darkness vanquished
morning comes
comforter warms
day beckons
bed comfier
than the promise
of fresh starts.

dreams

to take.

// 143

dreams are knocking on my eyelids.
they are getting impatient.

// 12

late night
lie awake
eyes open
dreams to take.

// 74

I often wonder why I
care so fucking much
why I love too hard
and fall too fast
why I let myself get hurt
so quickly
immediately
repeatedly.
and then I realize that
the opposite is worse
feelings at a standstill
holding the world
an arm's length away
indifferent, cold, and critical
I'd rather be an inferno
than a frozen,
remorseless
icicle.

// 203

I'm sinking,
to the bottom.
I'm a nervous wreck
can't hold my breath this long.
never learned to
deep-sea dive.
maybe someone will
find this treasure chest
of mine.

// 171

sometimes I forget
how lucky I am
to be lonely
since it means
I have people in my life
I can't wait
to spend
time with.

// 170

I am worth
so much more
than I let myself
believe.

// 136

at least
you'll have a poem
to show for it.

// 137

don't you ever think
that it was for
lack of trying.

// 202

isn't it funny
how home
has nothing to do
with place
instead it's about people
love, laughter
and grace.

// 201

a long time ago
in another life
I told my therapist
that I write poems
to deal with the sad
and it makes me feel ok
she asked
why don't you write
when you feel ok
and then maybe
you'll finally
feel happy.

you know what?
she was right.

// 28

the wind tickles my ear
it's trying to tell me something
but we don't speak the same language

// **128**

I didn't know the
world had this much oxygen

I can breathe again.

// **82**

it's easy to make
everyone a villain
when you only
see yourself as
the protagonist

// 92

someone asked me
"how's it going"
and normally,
honestly,
I hate small talk
with a burning passion
but today was different
because my answer changed
I was no longer
"ok" or "alright" or
"doing just fine"
but "fantastic"
"great" and for the first time
in a long while
I truthfully answered
"happy."

// **127**

sometimes
all you can do
is sleep
and hope
for a
better tomorrow.

// 86

the darkness was big today
so vast it encompassed me
a friend told me I seemed small
I wanted to tell her that's because
I was thousands of miles away.
she noticed that my
personality had shrunk
and no one has ever
noticed that before.

it felt so good
to be noticed.

// 64

tonight, I saw the
pitch black street light
moving too fast somewhere to be
midnight cityscape
reflected in my bedroom mirror
and I smiled because if its sheer beauty.

do you know how long it's been
since I smiled for me.

// 205

I haven't used the word 'giddy'
in a while.

I think I'm adding it
to my vocabulary.

//

I wrote this for you.

// 72

to the girl wondering when
she'll feel like 'herself' again,
remember
people who care about you
will love you no matter
the version of yourself
you choose to portray
they'll take furrowed brows
over fake smiles
downturned mouths
over cancelled plans
any day.

// 94

believe that you
do your best
because right now
even though it seems
like you offer half,
one quarter,
one teaspoon,
when everyone else is
able to give a gallon
remember that
they don't have to
fight for every drop
so claim your victories
recognize that
some days
just breathing
is a cause for
celebration.

// 132

to the girl who forgets to smile:
even though sadness
always finds its
home in you
and joy is
simply a visitor
this doesn't make
your body
a hostel for tears.
remember
to make friends
with your neighbors
when you hear laughter
drifting from the window
and don't forget
to leave the door
unlocked.

// 143

your fragility is breathtaking
don't let anyone tell you otherwise
it's just as beautiful as the sunrise in the east
sunset in the west
embrace the tightness in your chest
it's what makes you human
trust me.

// 163

some of my favourite memories
are the moments of silence
I've spent with you
not needing to constantly
search for something
to fill the gaps.

after all,
some of the most peaceful places
are known for their stillness.

// 153

I'd much rather you compliment my words
rather than the way my lips look
when I speak them.

// **148**

sometimes
I'd rather pretend I'm happy
than talk to you
about the sad days
and that's
perfectly
ok.

// 142

and the sound
of family
is nostalgia
and hope
and happiness.

why do I scra... m...

nees...

...for you

...hile you remain

...scathed.

// 21

why do I scrape my knees
when I fall for you
while you remain
unscathed.

// 129

I see you
waiting with baited breath
holding all your love
with arms crossed
waiting to spend it
on someone else
but here's a thought
uncross those arms
and instead of using it
to protect
how about you
love yourself
instead.

// 2

sometimes I am reminded:
tenor voices of your tongue;
bustling cobblestone.
curved slouch;
posture of the crescent moon.
inky blackness seeps outward
spilled water
stains my memories
not a day goes by that isn't contaminated
a sickness spreading and infiltrating
when all I want to be is healed.

it's foggy outside.

// **83**

how to be an ally:
redirect the spotlight
stand outside of it
hand over the mic.
don't hog it.
it's not about you anymore.

// 145

and when you're not ready,
life decides to move on.

// 187

'nana' is a synonym
for long visits
and warm smiles.
chocolates in a drawer,
moccasins by the bed.
stories about glistening snow
and a husband's love.

I'll always wished I
had spent more time
with her.

tasting them on my lips
reminding me of the ocean
that you drowned me in

seeing you on your hands and knees
begging for me to take

// 30

you're not worth my tears
but why do I still feel them
rolling down my cheeks
tasting them on my lips
reminding me of the ocean
that you drowned me in.
if you come crawling back for forgiveness
I don't know if I'd have the will power to say no
I' be so tired of swimming
trying to keep my head above water
because ever since you left
it's the one picture in my mind
that gives me comfort
seeing you on your hands and knees
begging for me to take you back
yet all I can think of is the way
I scraped my knees falling
so hard and so fast.

// 191

I look forward to the times
when we're under the same roof
because sometimes I feel like
you grew up overnight
so here's to being sixteen
watching childhood fade
in the rear view mirror
but don't worry
no matter how many birthdays go by
you'll always be my younger sister.

// 37

just because my name is long
or hard to pronounce for your
anglophone tongue
doesn't make you the decider
or controller
or shortener
of the one thing that is my own.
you call me by a nickname
that I have told you
and told you
and told you
I dislike.
but you continue to use it
because to you, "It's cute" or you "like it" or
"it's so much easier to say"
in a world where
I don't even have the right to my own body
in a world where society tells me how to behave
how to be appreciated
in a world where my looks are the first thing
you see and sometimes the only thing
where my personality is glossed over
because my curves are the one thing
you're looking for.
a place where my first day of high school
my mother told me to "wear something normal"
to "make a good impression"
so that I wouldn't be laughed out of the building.
a place where by the ripe old age of thirteen
I started noticing men's looks changing
when they saw me.

"you're so cute" turned into "hey sexy"
and "hellos" turned into whistles
waves into catcalls.
I was taught by friends
to hold my keys in a death grip
I was shown videos
with the other girls in my class
on when to kick and where to punch
and how loud to scream
If I was ever followed alone at night
you see
just because you're a man
and you're used to getting your own way
doesn't mean you get to decide what to say
to make me follow you like a dog
I might seem like an innocent puppy
but my voice is loud and my arms are strong
I prefer the term wolf
because we run in packs
to circle our prey
we howl at the moon
and our collective voices
are louder than your one
I'm tired of letting other people like you
use your male privilege to
decide my identity
so from now one
you better call me gabrielle
and not
gabby.

// 185

have you ever noticed
how airports make
time stand still.

not quite arrived,
when you haven't
quite left.

// 186

everyone laughs
in the same
language.

// 183

all mirrors do
is tell lies
if you want to know
what you truly look like
peer into your best
friend's eyes.

// 3

longing over glass
how do you miss someone you've never met
history of regret
absent voices frozen smile
speak from your thumbs
hear with my eyes
face to face wouldn't recognize.

// 56

remember how my words were soft
while yours cut me with their
rough edges and careless corners
remember how you told me
that I made you a better person?
that was a one sided statement
the feeling was not mutual
I was the hot air balloon
you were the bags of sand
constantly trying to drag
me to the ground.
a rope that tethered me home
when all I wanted
was to leave that place behind.

and to think I almost stayed
for the likes of you.

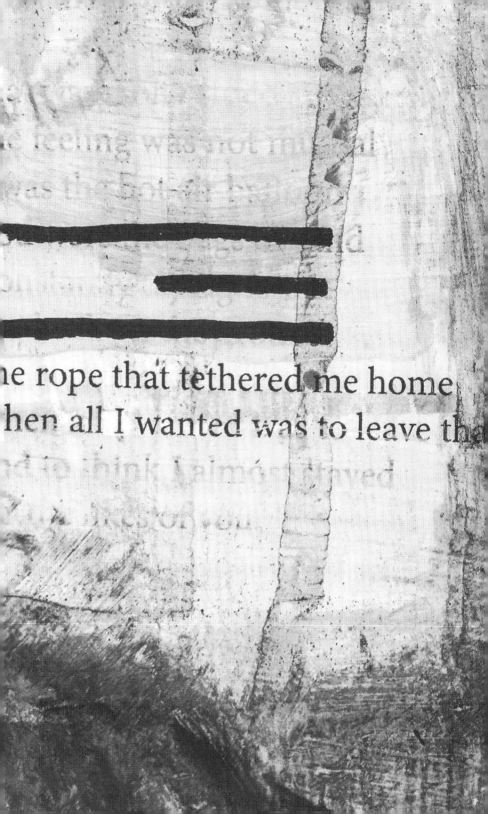

e rope that tethered me home
hen all I wanted was to leave tha

// 38

I've been thinking about you lately
but I swear my brain is
playing tricks
It's only remembering
the good times
and pretending the bad times
didn't exist

idn't exist.

... my hea

... me, you ...

...etimes I can't l...

...t doesn't me...

...ening.

// 55

sometimes my head is too noisy
sometimes your voice is too soft
sometimes I can't hear you
but that doesn't mean
I'm not listening.

// **113**

love yourself
even when it
seems impossible.
that's when you
need love
the most.

// 6

the bell laughs in my face
ringing ringing
sounds like you
once did
forever
in the future
ago.

// 42

voice brimming with promise
future vast as pink sky
but the sun wasn't rising
we were the winter solstice
cold dark and
emotionless

// 39

I've been feeling
uninspired lately
and when I wondered
to myself
why that was
I realized
that it's because
I'm finally over
you.

// 34

sometimes I hate
the way I need you
to remind me
to love myself.

sometimes I hate
the way I need you

to remind me

to love myself

// 48

he and I were fireworks,
over before the camera could flash,
before you could capture the picture
of romance.
we are slow burning
kindling
glowing ember
a spark that quickly turned
into a forest fire
engulfing everything around us in flames
a fire that takes over all of its surroundings
he was explosive
fireworks that turned into butterflies
that lit up the night skies
just a fraction of a second
you blink and they are gone
we are the forest fire
smoke that enters your lungs
reminds yourself that you can't breathe
when he's around
leaves you gasping for air
a passion that isn't going anywhere
no one can put us out.

...ng embe...

...rk that quickly tu...

a forest fire

...fing everythin...

...hat takes ove... ...ll of...

...s explosive

...s that tur... ...into...

...up the r...

...inactie...

...link

// 43

I missed this
the
laying in the couch
you at the desk
sister's legs folded
dad somewhere
in the background
dog at my feet
giving me literal
puppy dog eyes
sounds from a tv show
resonating like drums
in the distance
rumbling of the train
on the tracks
off to the middle
of nowhere
or maybe somewhere
none of us speaking
to each other
just enjoying the presence
of one another
comforting silence
one that needs not
be broken
a silence that yells
a whisper that all can hear
if you listen it is shouting
"we are family"
and
"you are home."

// 140

why do I allow
other people
to make me feel
utterly worthless
why do I allow
you
to make me think
I'm not worth your
time.
because I am worth
centuries
yet I keep hoping
for just a few more
of your
seconds.

// 29

we're like a teeter totter
one moment I'm up
one moment I'm down
but as soon as you leave
I'm on the ground

// 103

all I needed was an apology
but I guess the word 'sorry'
wasn't in your vocabulary.

//

I wrote this for me.

// 164

sometimes I feel like
I don't have a lot to say.
and I have to remind myself
that it's ok
to be a wallflower
rather than
a centerpiece.

// 100

I need to remember
that I've never
wasted my love
not one drop
maybe I should have
redirected it,
inwards
but who knows
they probably
needed it more
than I did.

// 124

if my head
was a house
my backyard is a
broken down fence
overgrown weeds
yours has
white picket posts
and evenly spaced trees.
I'd like to think
mine is charming
in its decrepitness
but yours is
as perfect
as it is
pristine.

// 122

I wore three inch heels tonight
making me taller than
five foot nine
but when I stood
in the way of a streetlight
my shadow was
twenty feet tall and
three feet wide.

no wonder I feel most
powerful at night.

// 195

chronic night owl
daytime couch sleeper
music playlist maker
subtitle movie reader
forgot about my tea now it's cold drinker
unrelenting procrastinator.
can you tell I'm an over-thinker?

// 190

sometimes I look in the mirror
and think
damn
isn't she gorgeous
now if only I could
stop staying it
in the third person.

// 190

sometimes I look in the mirror
and think
damn
isn't she gorgeous
now if only I could
stop staying it
in the third person.

// 150

you didn't ask for this
I repeat
over
and
over
again.

// 146

I have so
many more
words
inside of
me.

// 182

lately,
I've realized
that I'm patient with everyone
but myself.

// 181

sometimes I forget to water
the garden
that is me.

// **168**

today I took my journal
out of hiding
I've been too comfortable
looking at it on my bookshelf
reminding me of all
the words stuck inside
looking for a way out.

// 189

right now I'm
testing the waters
navigating unsteadiness
because you know what they say
a silent sea never made
skillful sailors.

// 7

how do you whisper loudly
no one showed me how
how do you laugh quietly
no one ever taught me
how do you sleep soundly
my dreams make too much noise
how do you read quickly
the words stick to the back of my eyes
how do you listen attentively
when there is so much to be heard
don't tell me how to live
I think that's

just absurd.

// 91

there is going to be something
that makes the struggle worth it.
there has to be.

// 169

sometimes my wardrobe
feels like a costume
for this character I played
centuries ago.
I wonder what that girl
would think
of who
she's become.

// 184

I need to stop apologizing
for taking up too much space
no one ever puts the
shrinking violet in the vase.

// 139

why do I try
to be kind
to everyone
but myself.

// 135

in the future
I'll wish I had
demanded
more
kindness.

// 80

I'm writing again.
saying
"welcome home, stranger"
to my brain.

// 90

I guess feeling everything
is better than feeling
nothing at all.

// 178

watering my plants give me comfort
because it's a reminder that
if I can keep them alive
I can do the same thing
with myself.

// **116**

I should really
start listening to
the advice
I give
to others.

// 138

pounding temples
make hearing
my voice
impossible.
good thing
I can read
my own lips.

// 108

I'm ready
for someone to love
every part of me
whose hands caress
instead of scold
whose tongue
professes
rather than holds
I'm ready
for that person
to be me.

// 120

when everyone's asleep
when the air is still
when the streets are quiet
and all I hear
is a fan whirring
softly breathing
rainwater trickling
that's when the thoughts
in my head
are the loudest.

// 152

things I'm really good at:
being impatient
falling in love with the wrong boy
tapping my foot
trying six different outfits
before deciding
on the t shirt I wore yesterday
leaving dirty dishes in the sink
and emails unopened
falling asleep on the couch
forgetting to brush my teeth
taking my pills
remembering my mom's birthday
noticing someone else's sadness
mainly because I've had a lot
of practice
at noticing
my own.

// **110**

I'm tired of waiting
for someone to care
I'm tired of waiting
for that person
to be me.

// 1

I guess I feel like I have a lot to say
but then when I open my mouth the words
just kind of
stay there
empty
still
and in my head they're white water,
long rapids
heading towards the falls.
but when I speak they're
drops of condensation on a foggy mirror
easily erased
slowly trickling

I think people underestimate me.

// 200

how infuriating is it
that men find it their
obligation
to tell me I'm pretty
as though I didn't
already
know it.

// 95

the less I write
the more the words get jumbled
the less I write down
the more they just seem to fall out.

// 88

I'm still looking for my voice
and that's ok.

// **89**

one day I'm going
to share these words
with someone else.

// 176

what's most comforting
is knowing my best words
are still in front of me.

// 174

neither here nor there
complexion in between
raven hair
settler's skin
whose land do
I reside in.

// 206

note to self:

you don't have to pretend
that everything is fine.
even the people who
look like they have
it all together
have moments like this.

//

for the eyes.

ve the world.

Annie Leibovitz

the guise

Loving

been able

love as?

is

painful

loving is painful.

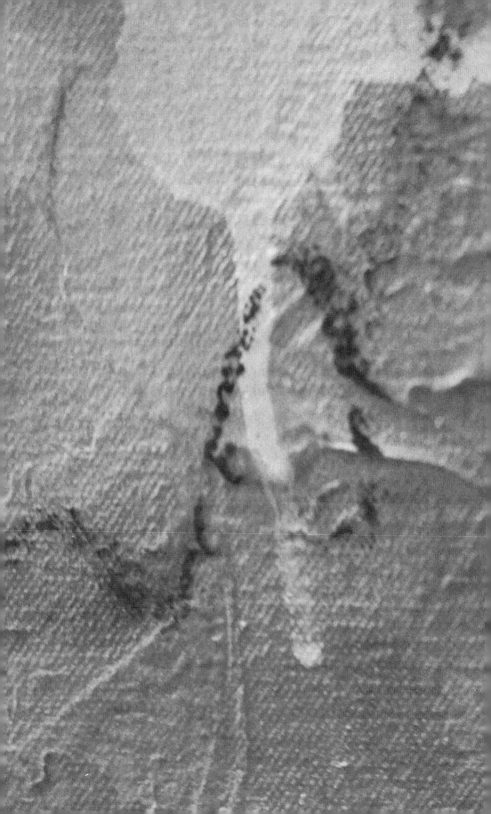

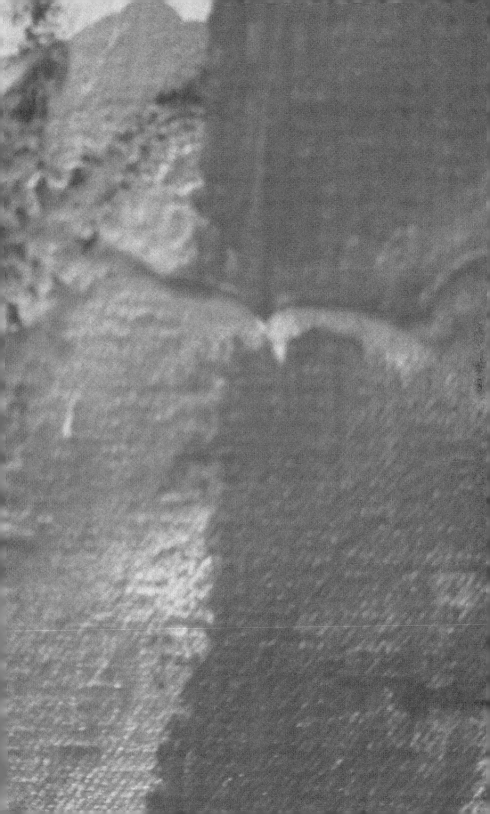

r **you have raised me up.**

I will extol you O Lord, for you have
drawn me
and did not let my foes rejoice.
Lord, you brought up my soul
you raised me to life from among
down · to the Pit.

Sing praises
his · faith

432

blackout poem #5

sur

moment with your eyes
yourself appr
another person. At the
ve, as if it were a cumbersom
e, fear,
om expressing your authenticity
nce the freedom of
true self.

I have the courage to be myself.

I trust

I trust.

DOCTOR

COLLECT

mortal frailty

reigns

depression is anger.

Depression

is anger.

who is she.

strength.

... courage ... fear is ... be avoided, but ... through ... from. Every ... we face a fear and walk into the middle ... support ... little bit is ... Continually having the courage ... internal dragons of our fears frees us ... living reactively and gives us the oppor- ... nity to be who we truly are.

strength is courage.

ON™

ALERIA

ACRYLIC™

TITANIUM WHITE

BLANC DE TITANE

BLANCO DE TITANIO

BIANCO DI TITANIO

TITANWEISS

Series/Série/Serie 1

200ml ℮
6.75 US fl

TOXIC

//

fin.

//

acknowledgments.

thank you.

to dr. mowat who not only saved my life but gave me one worth living.

to the professors who supported me, and taught me about typography and kerning and colour theory.

to izz and r who keep me humble with their honestly, which makes their praise so much more worthwhile.

to mom and dad. for your support. but mostly for always being proud of me, even for when I didn't deserve it.

grandpa, thank you for showing me glimpses of your soul written down in words.

grandma, thank you for reminding him to show me.

hales. thank you for being you. thank you for your love, which I don't reciprocate enough.

k-z. thank you for sticking around no matter how many miles separate us.

to k and k. thank you for the friendship, thc cocktails, and the board game nights.

and finally, to all the friends and family who convinced me that my work was good enough to turn into a book.

you're the reason I'm here.

// g.l.

//

about the author.

Photo courtesy of the U of A B.Des Grad Committee of 2019

Gabrielle Lussier is an emerging artist and designer in the Edmonton region originally from northern Alberta. She completed her Bachelor of Fine Arts with Distinction at the University of Alberta in the spring of 2017, and is currently studying a Bachelor of Design in Visual Communication Design to be completed in April of 2019.

Through her fine art practice Gabrielle explores the relationships between medication, mental health, social media, femininity and grunge aesthetics through the lens of painting, performative poetry and video.

Gabrielle has exhibited in multiple exhibitions across Alberta, most recently her solo show "Navigating Unsteadiness" at the Centre for Creative Arts in Grande Prairie. Her most recent work is a translation of her current poetry practice through the medium of paint and collage dealing with obstruction and illegibility.

In her design practice Gabrielle enjoys branding, illustration and UI/UX design and is passionate about making design accessible to everyone. She also loves being able to incorporate her fine art background any way she can, whether that be with collage, illustration, or calligraphy.

To learn more about her, or to see more examples of work, you can visit www.gabriellelussier.com. Follow her personal instagram @gbrielle.olivia or her design account @gbrielle.creative.

37929979R00127

Made in the USA
Lexington, KY
02 May 2019